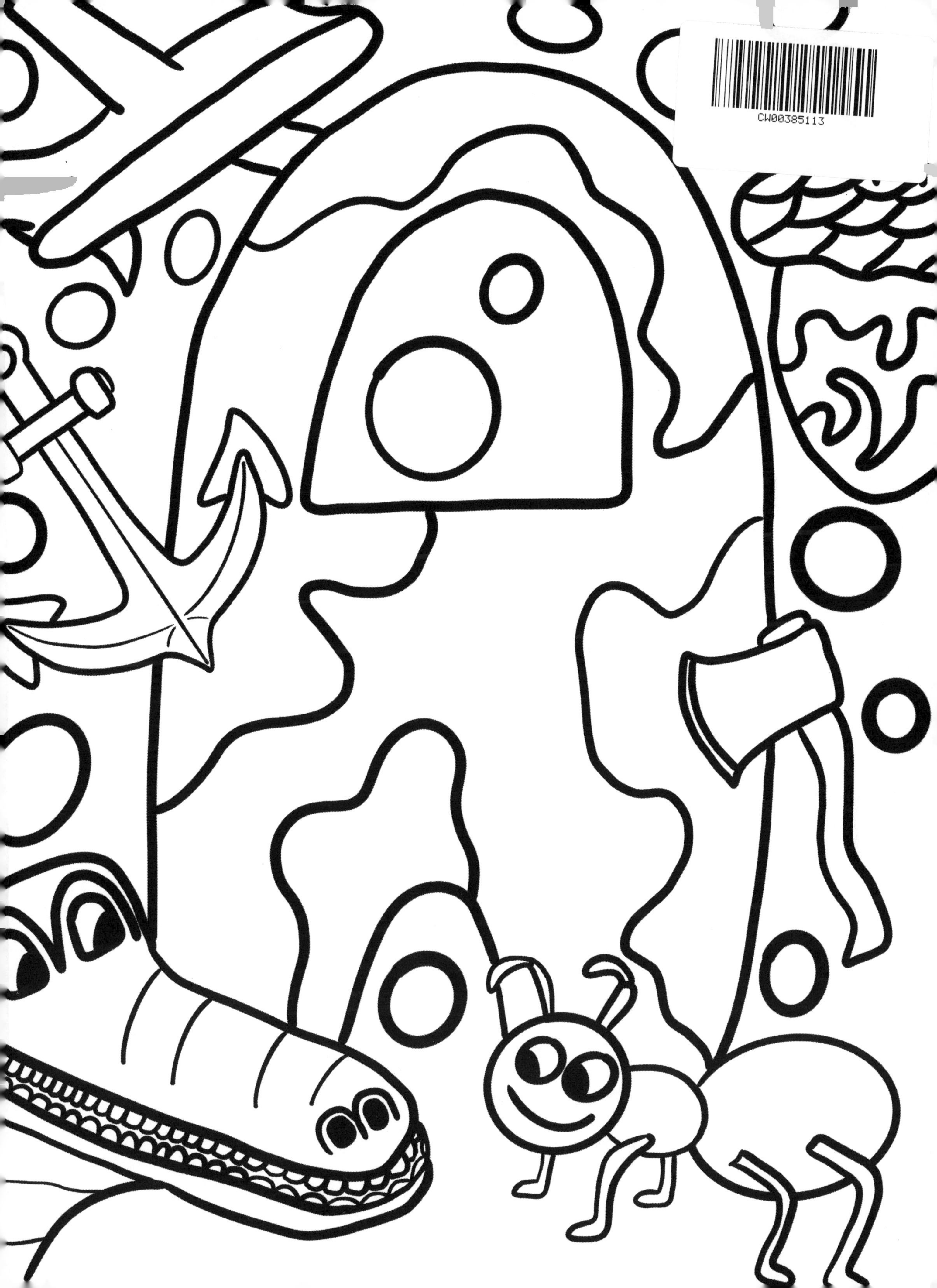

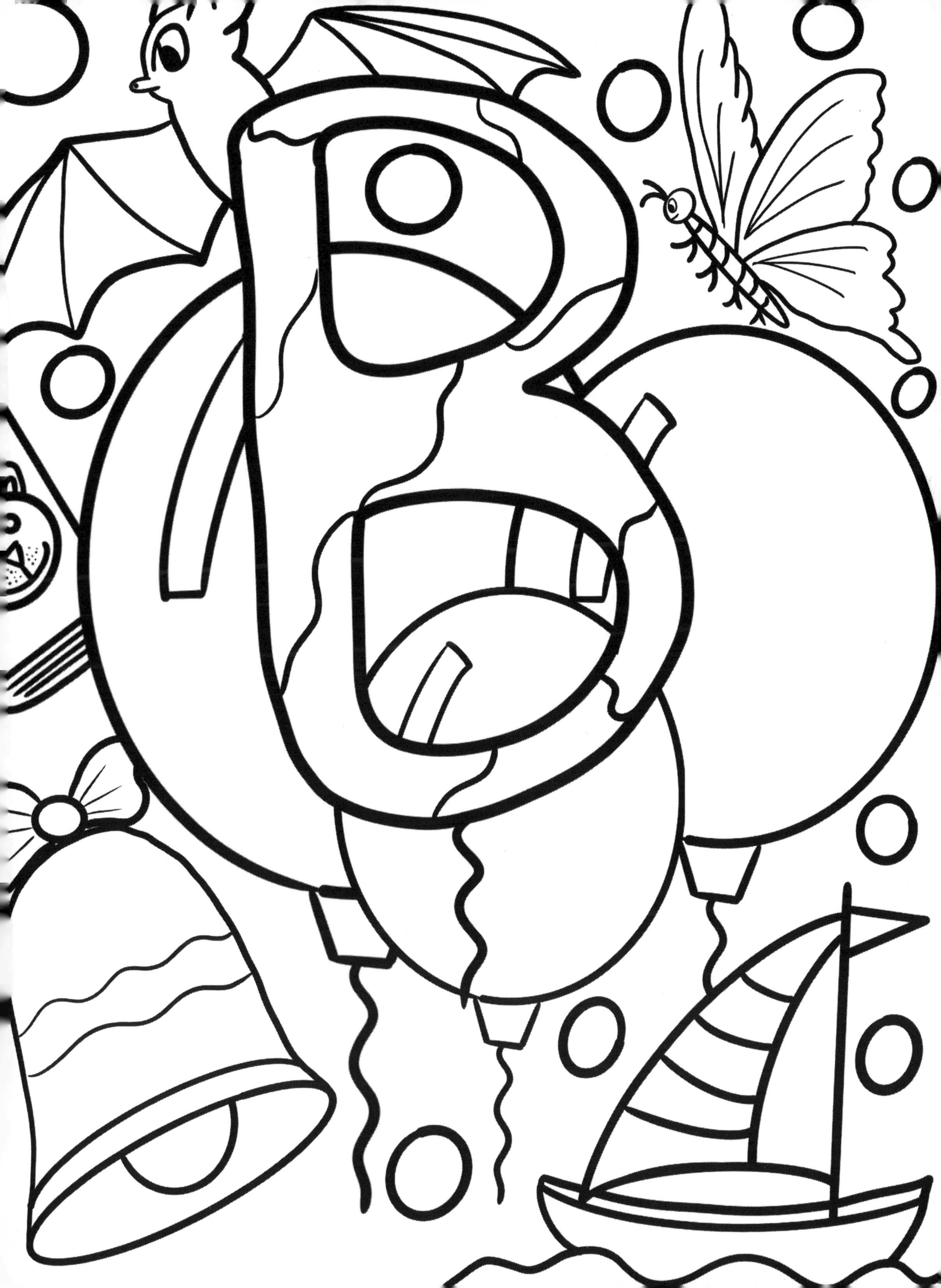

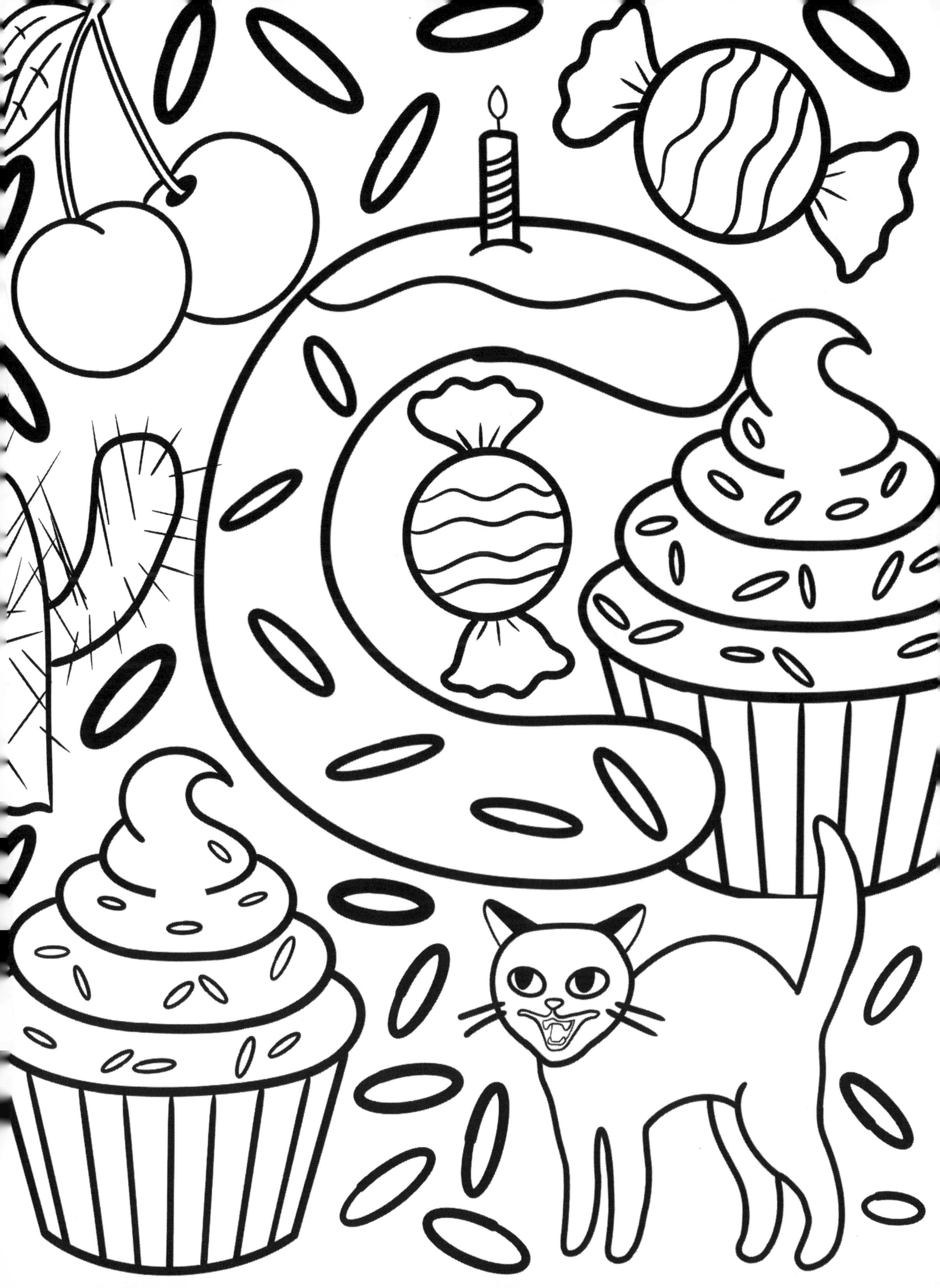

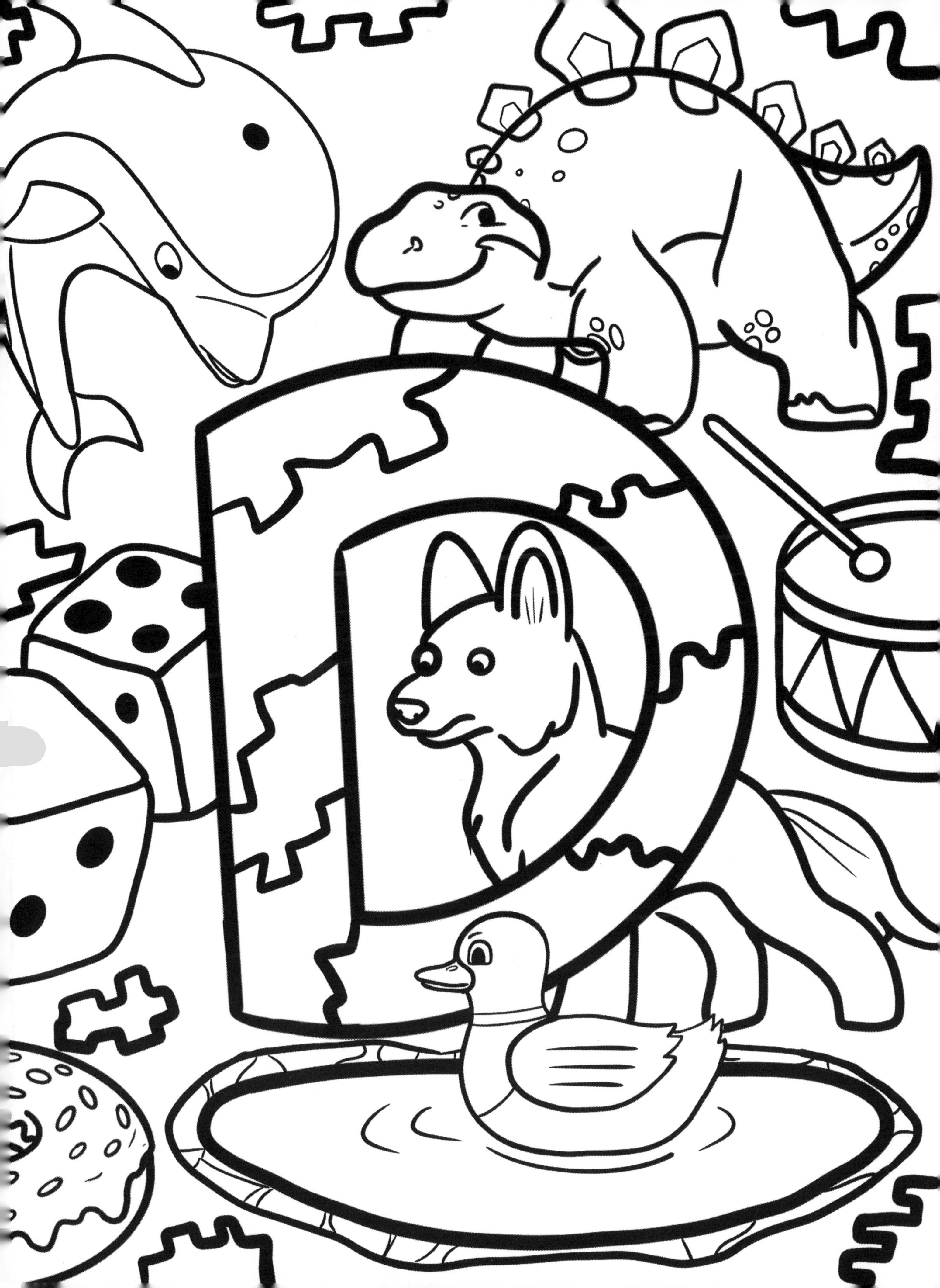

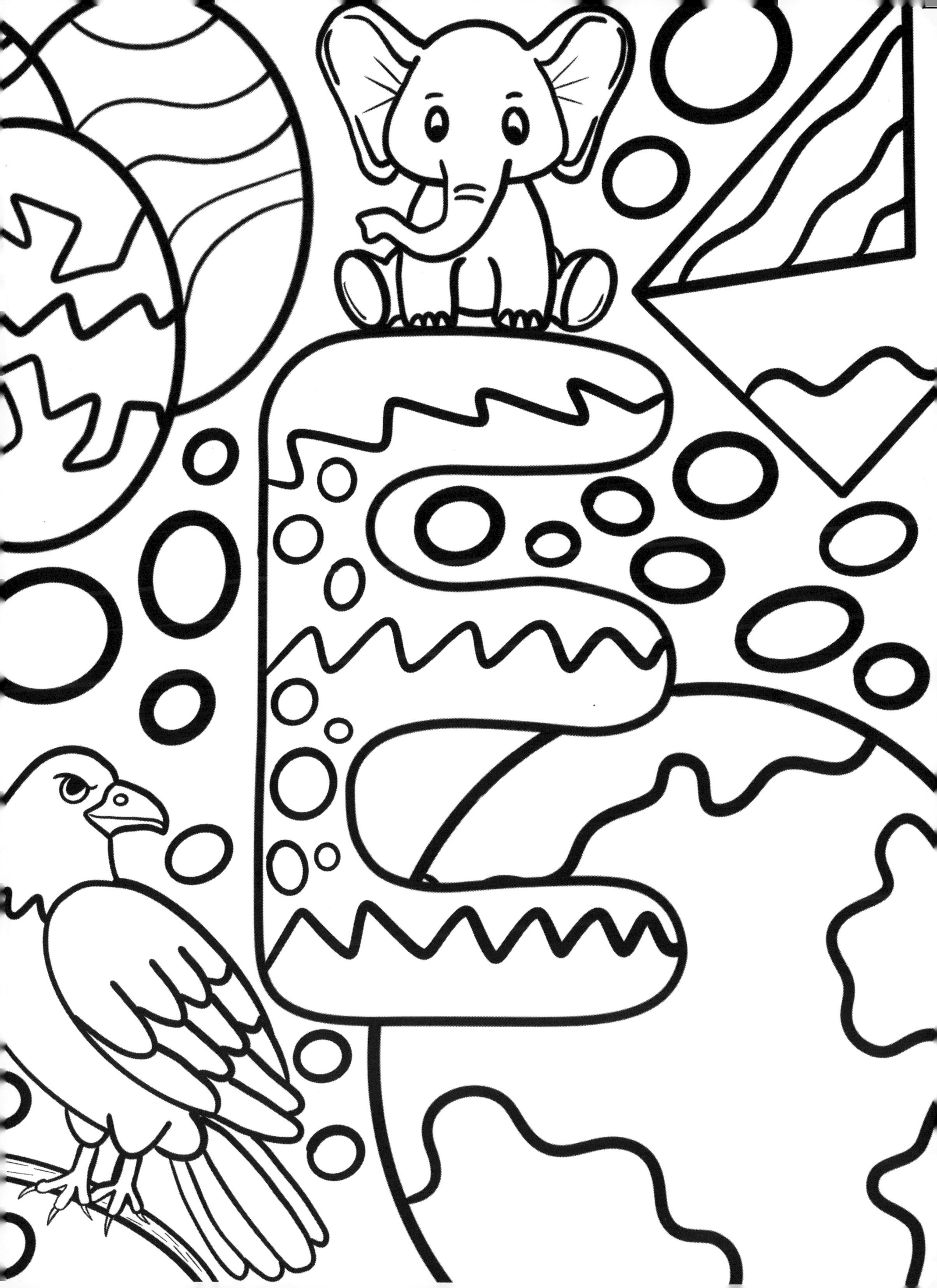

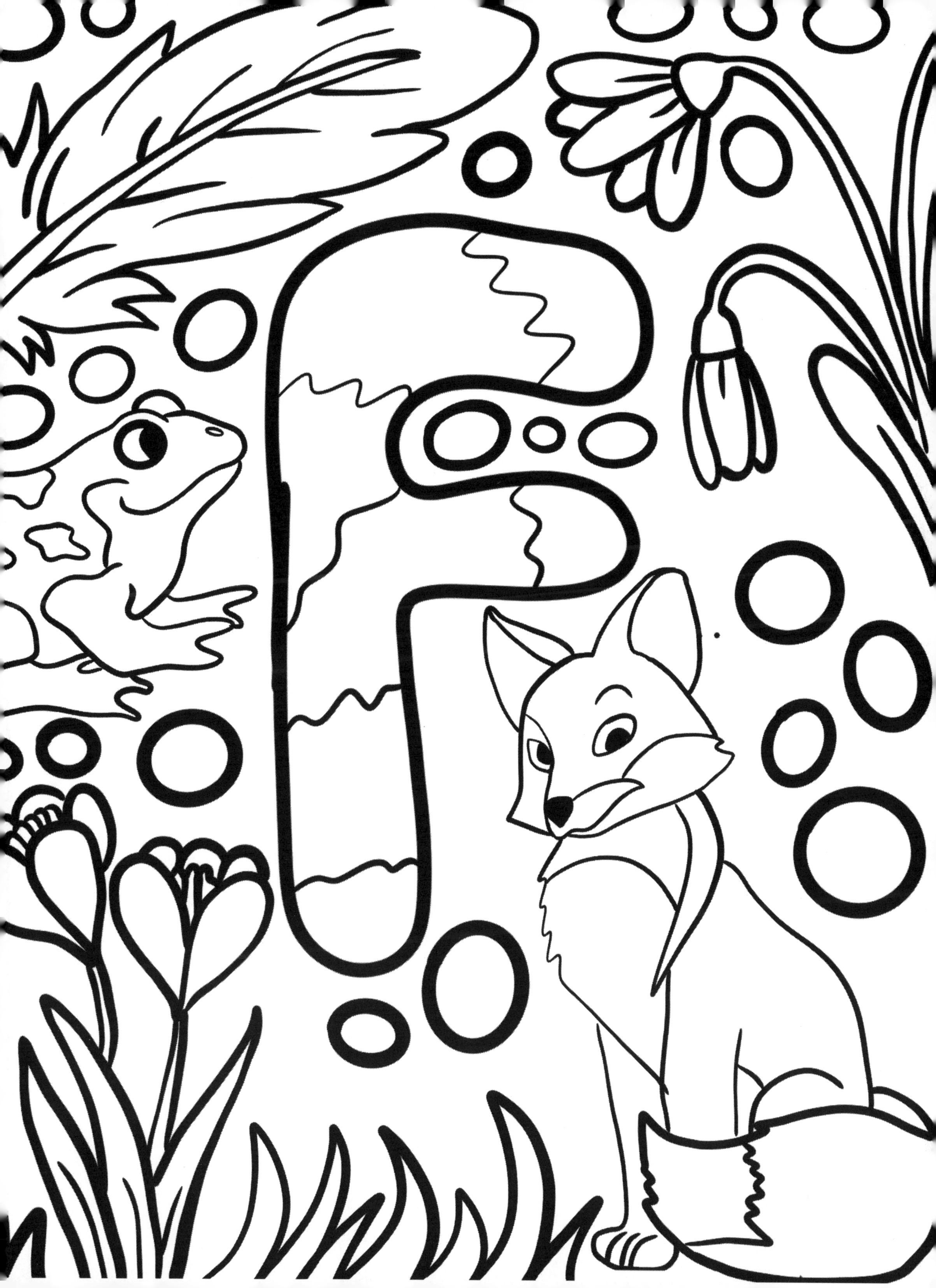

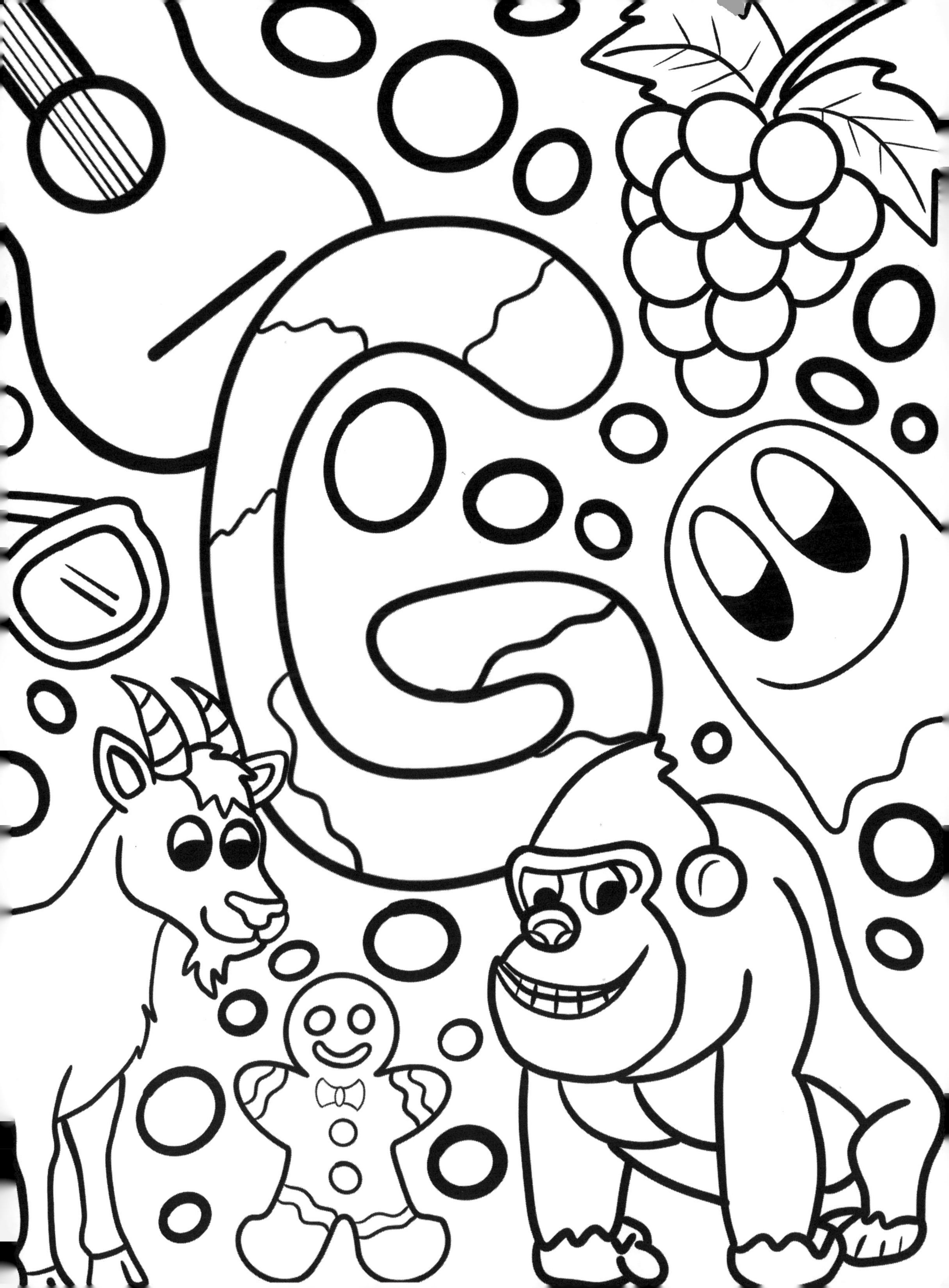

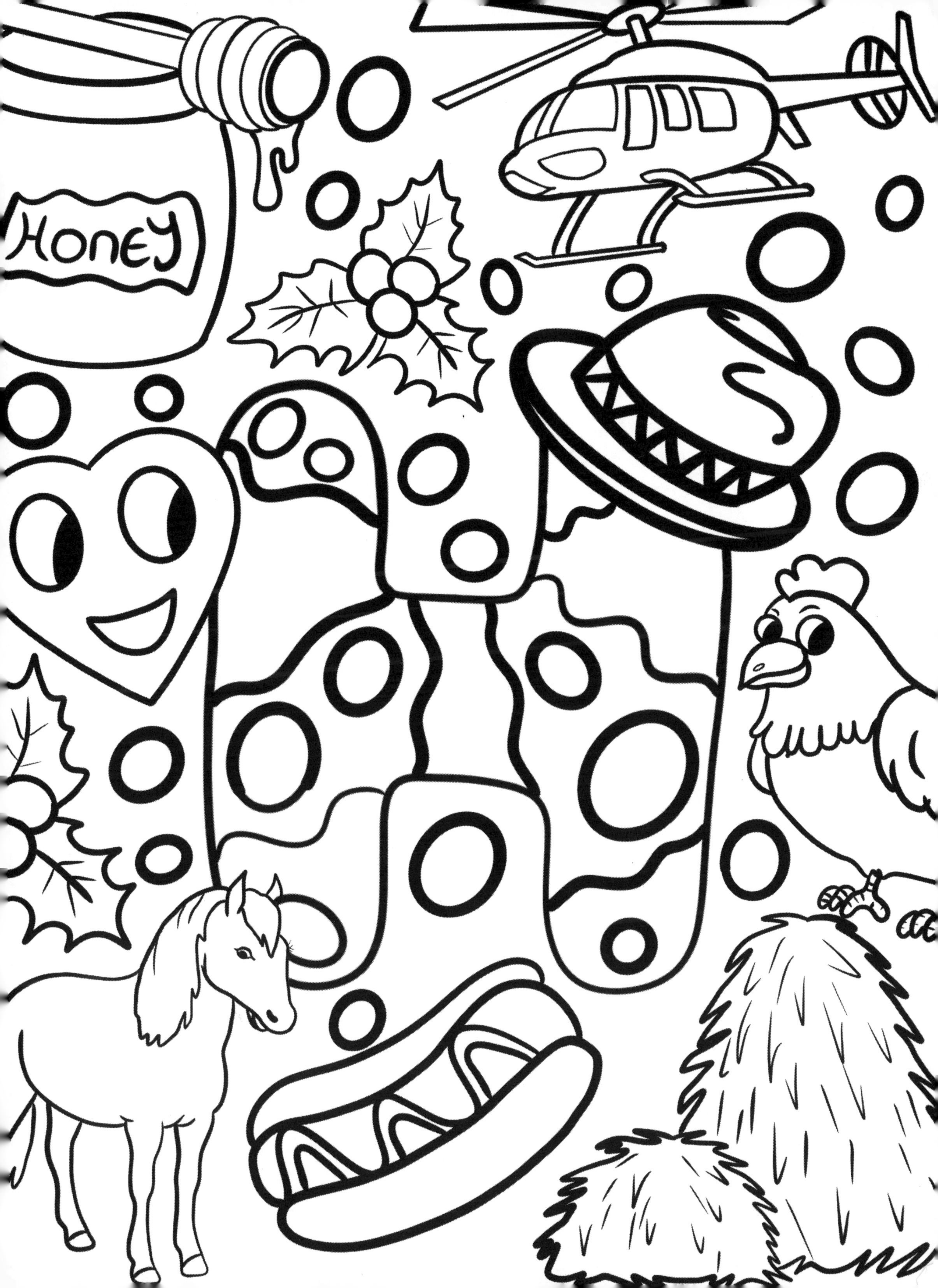
HONEY

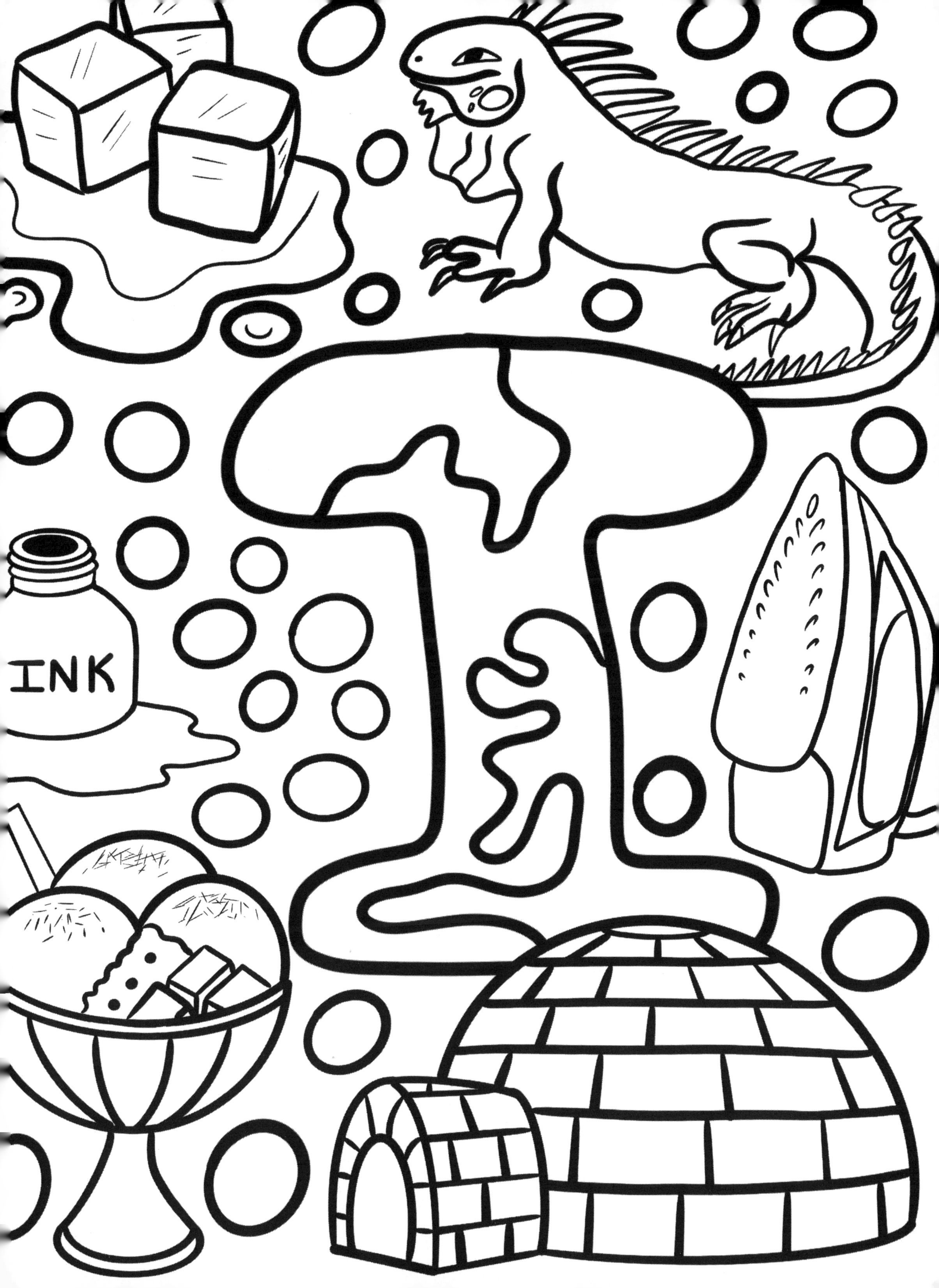
INK

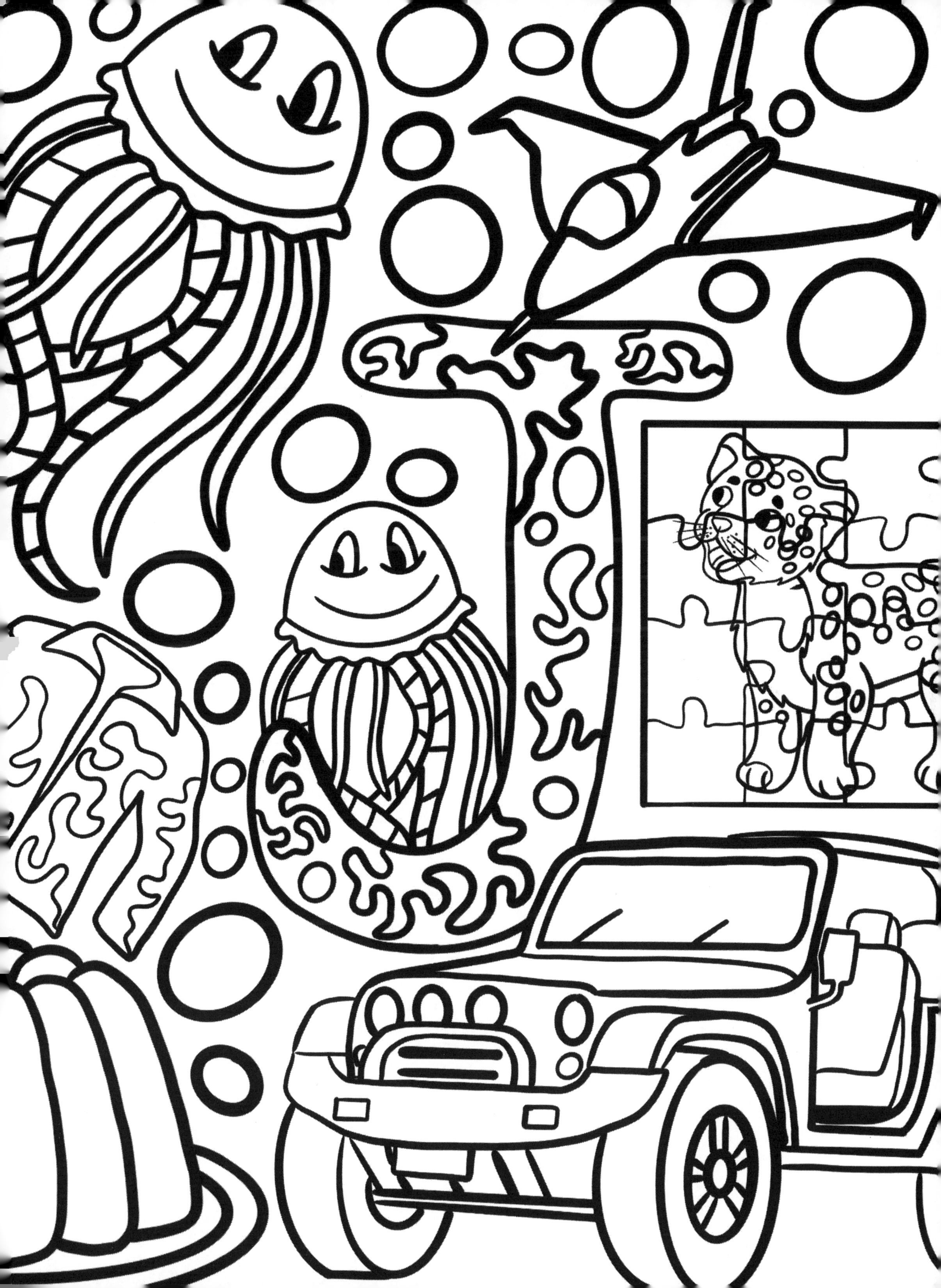

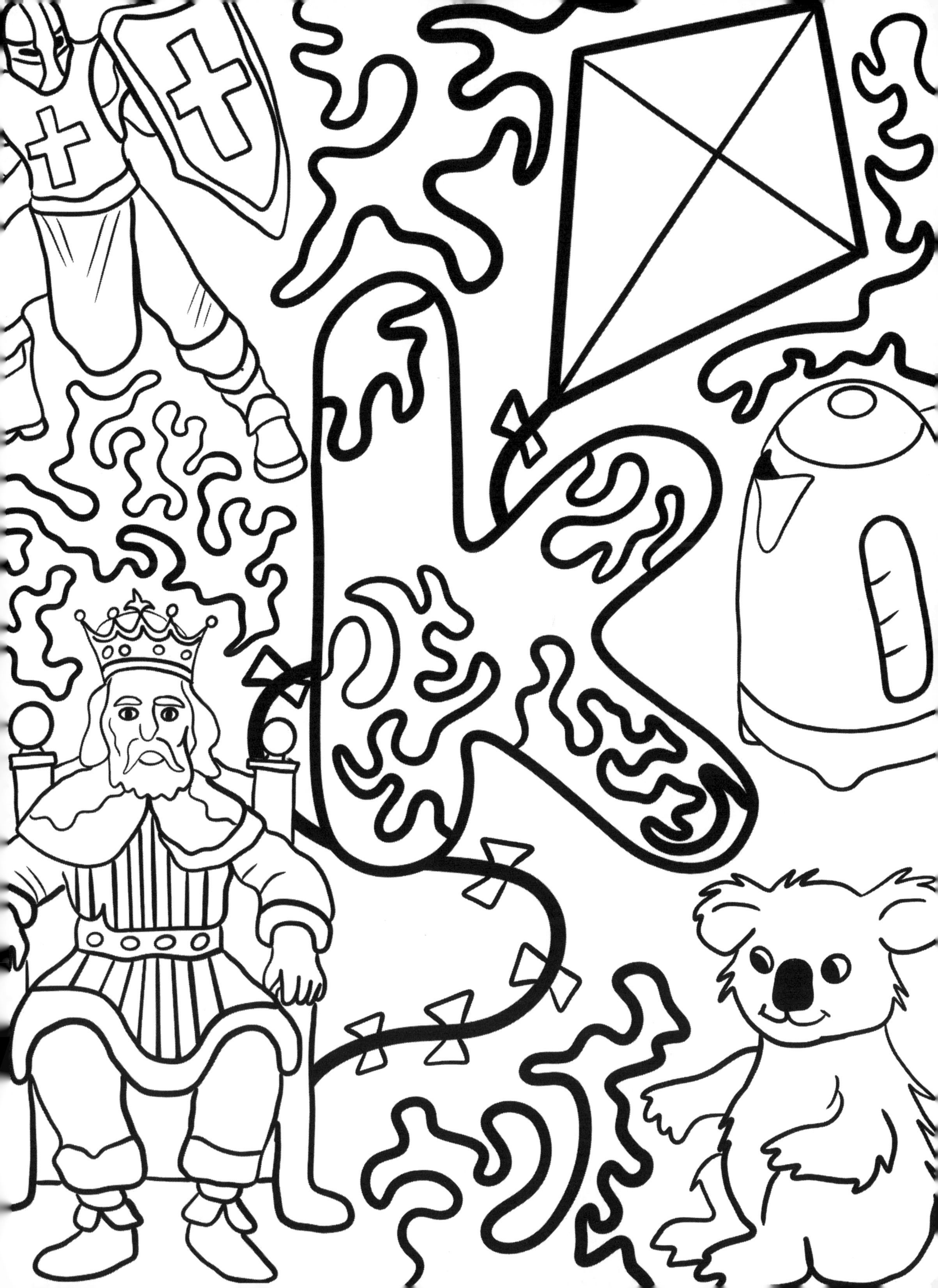

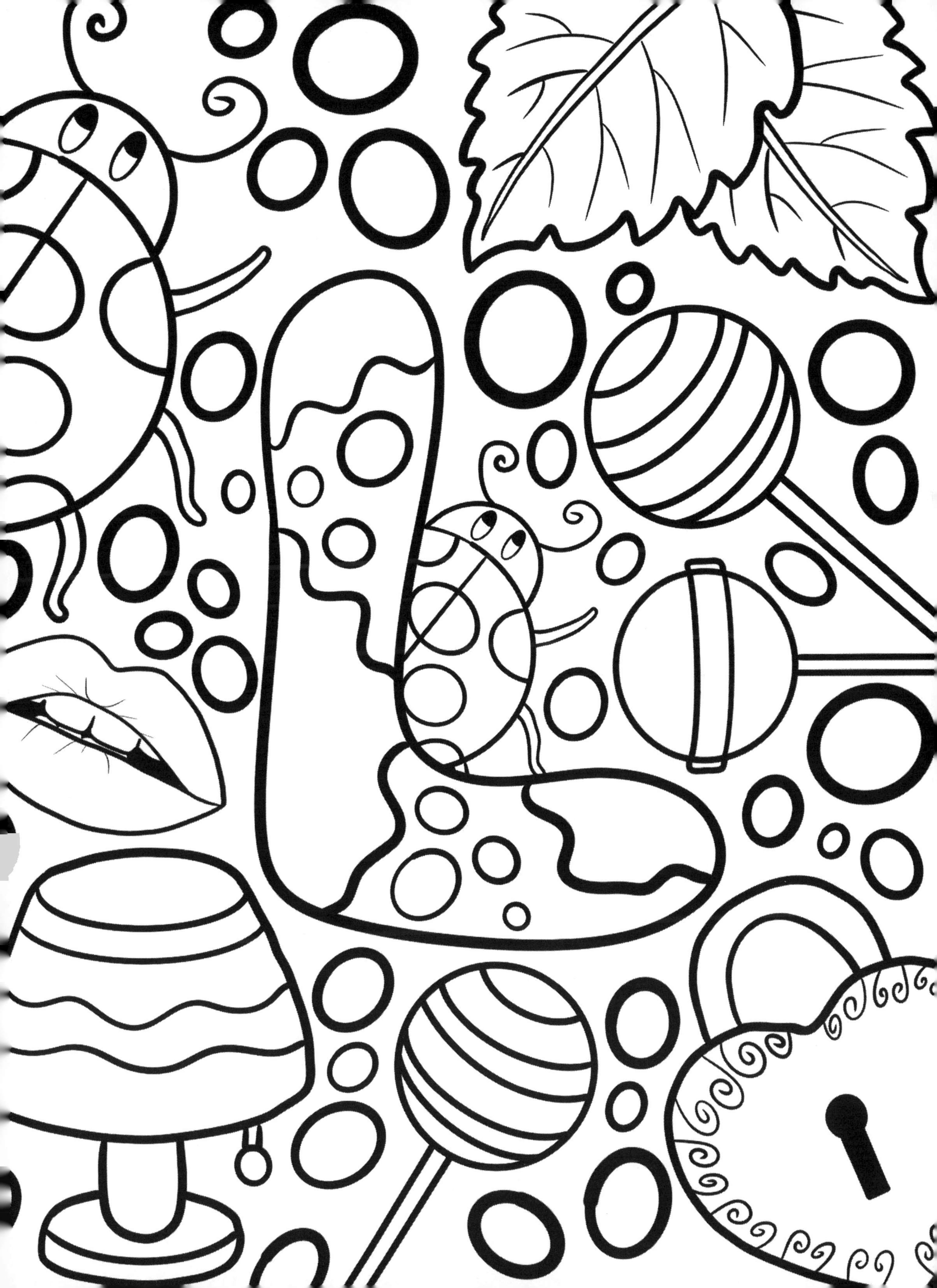

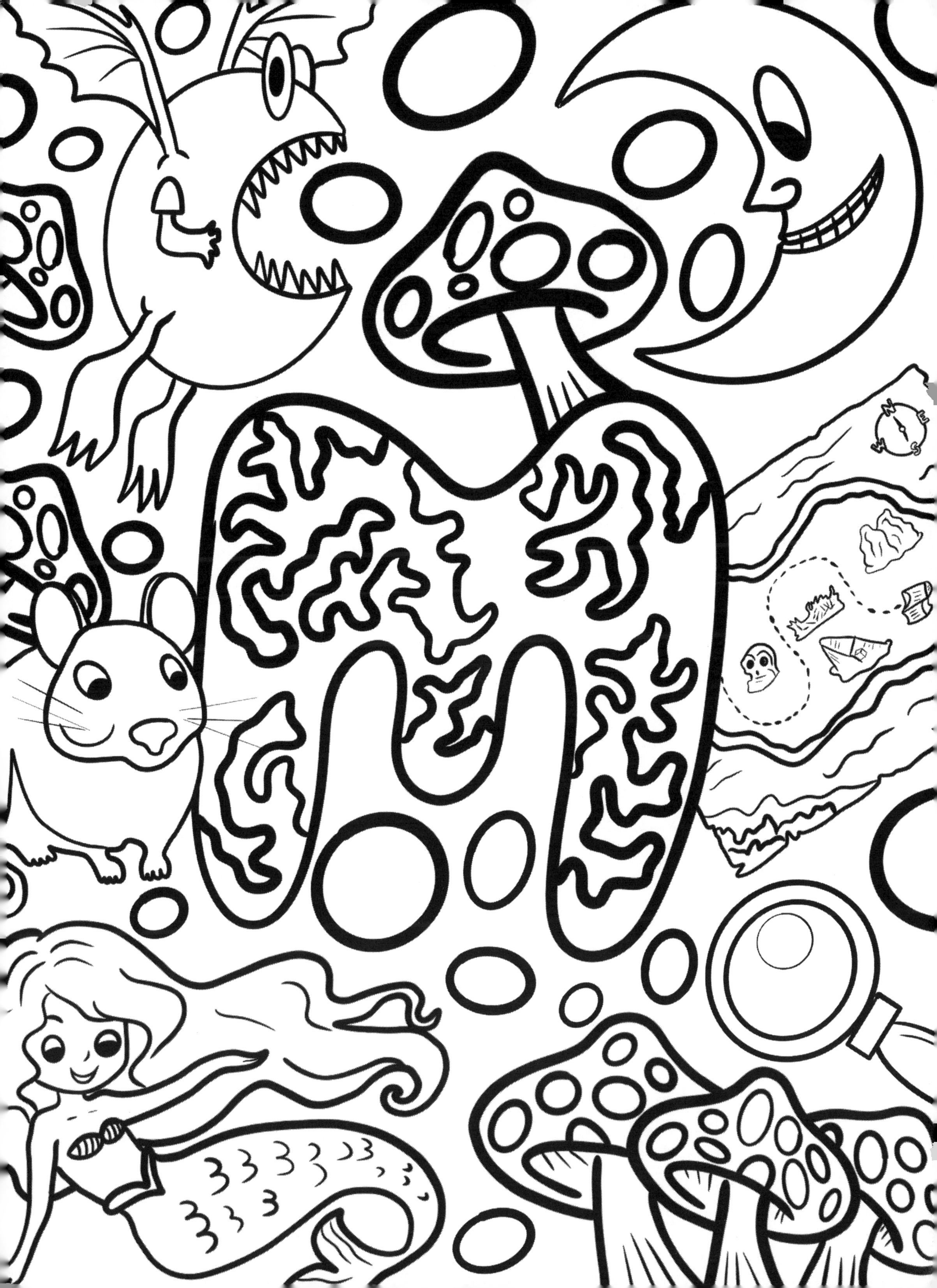

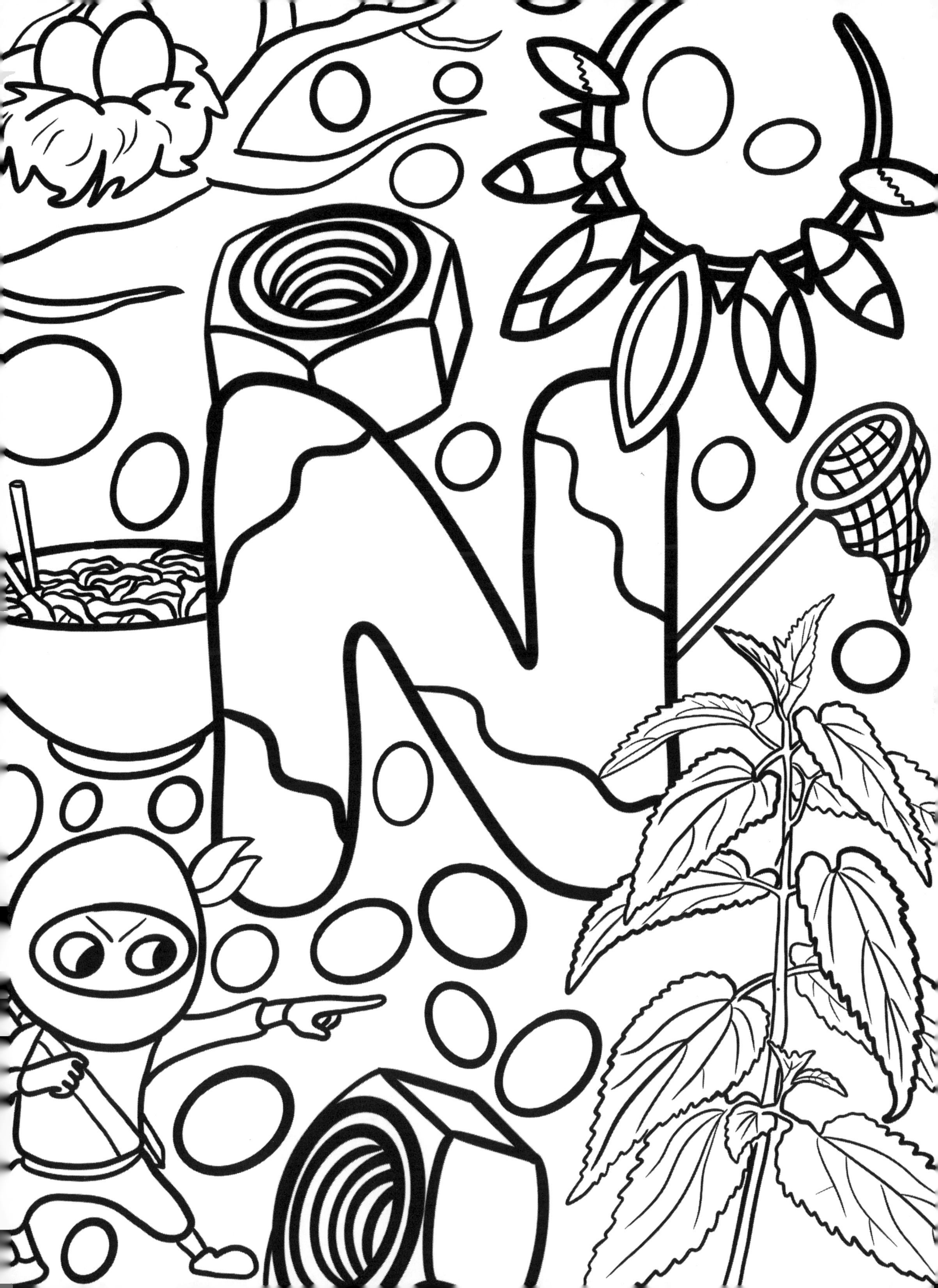

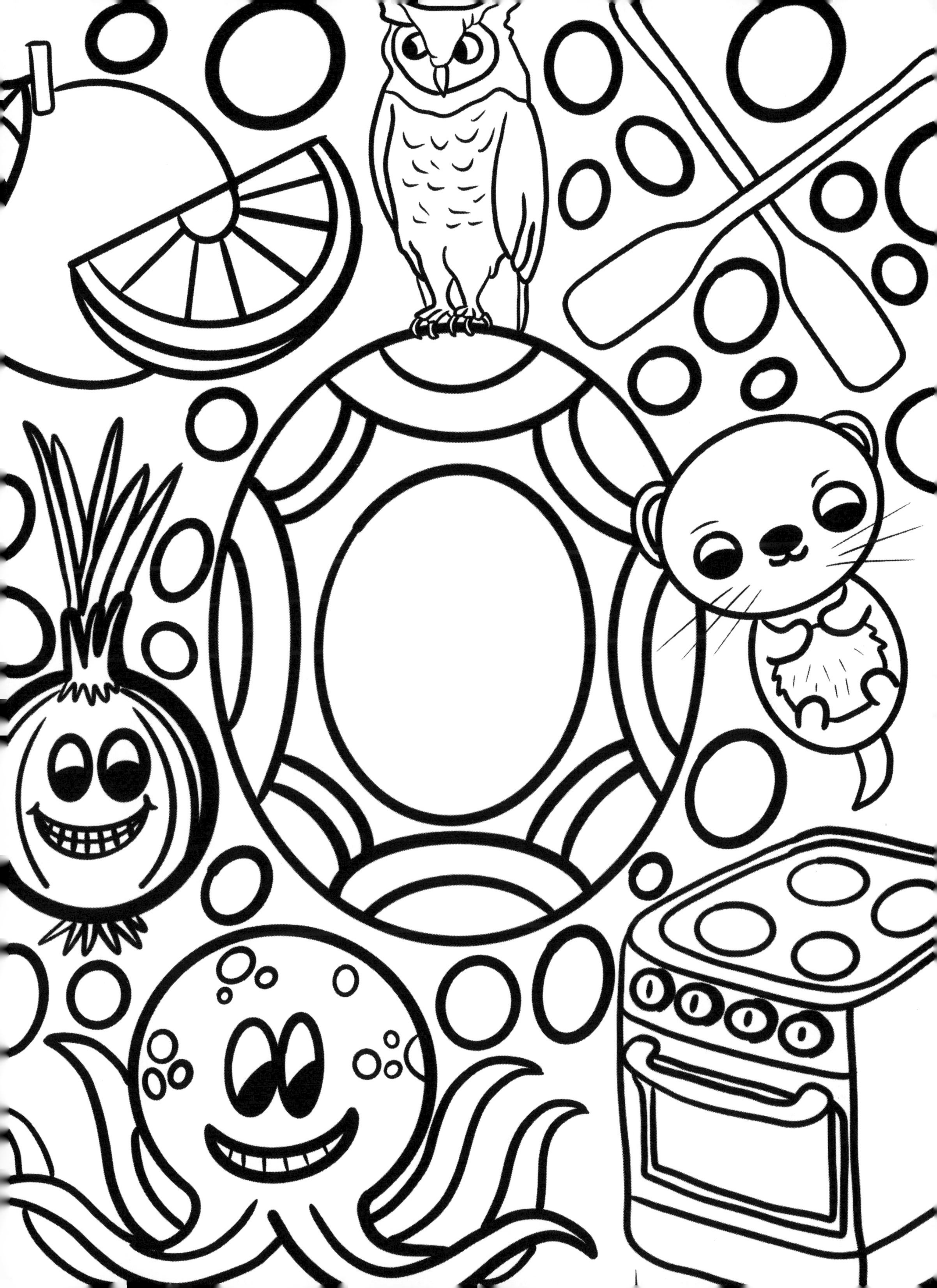

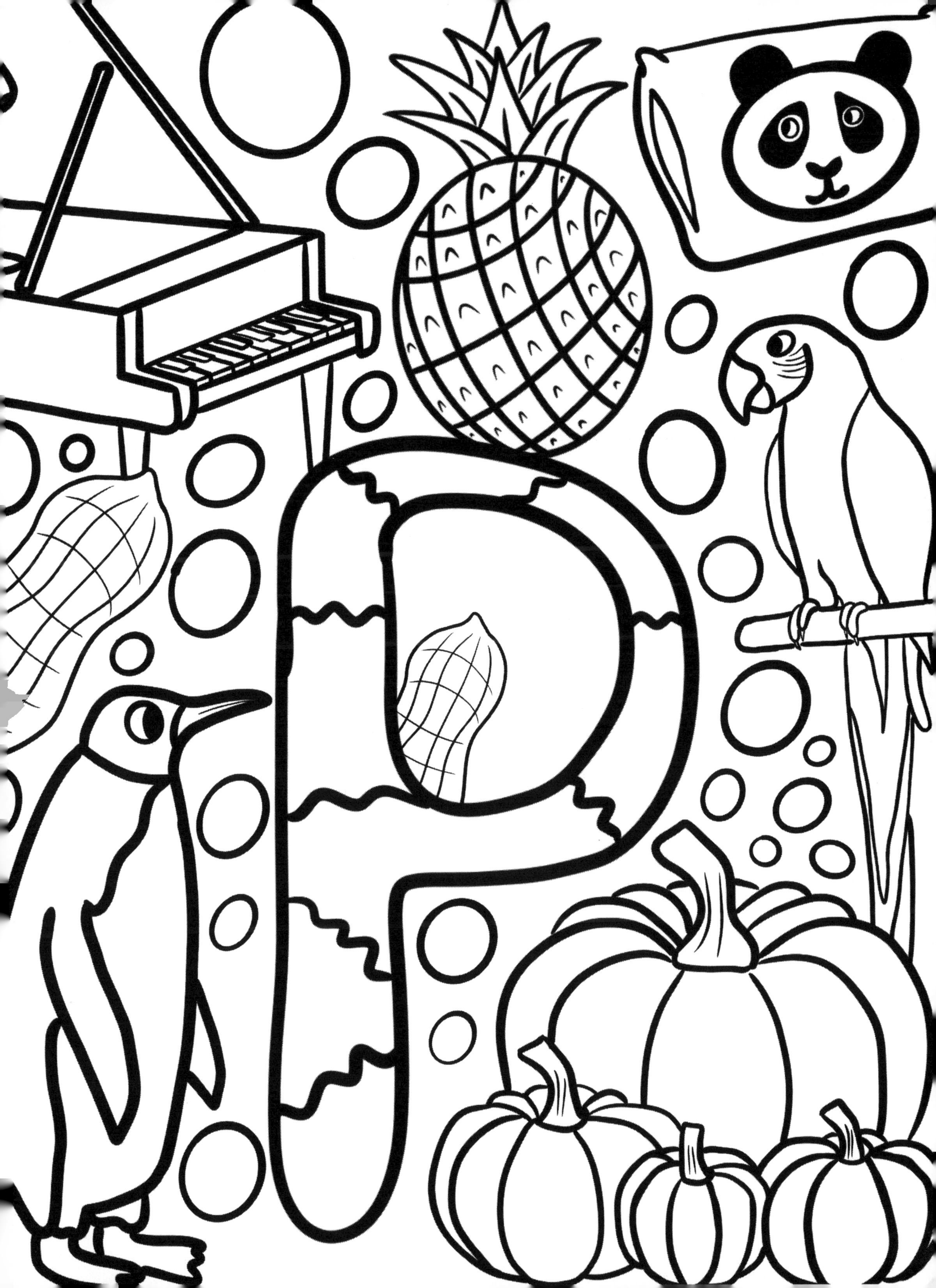

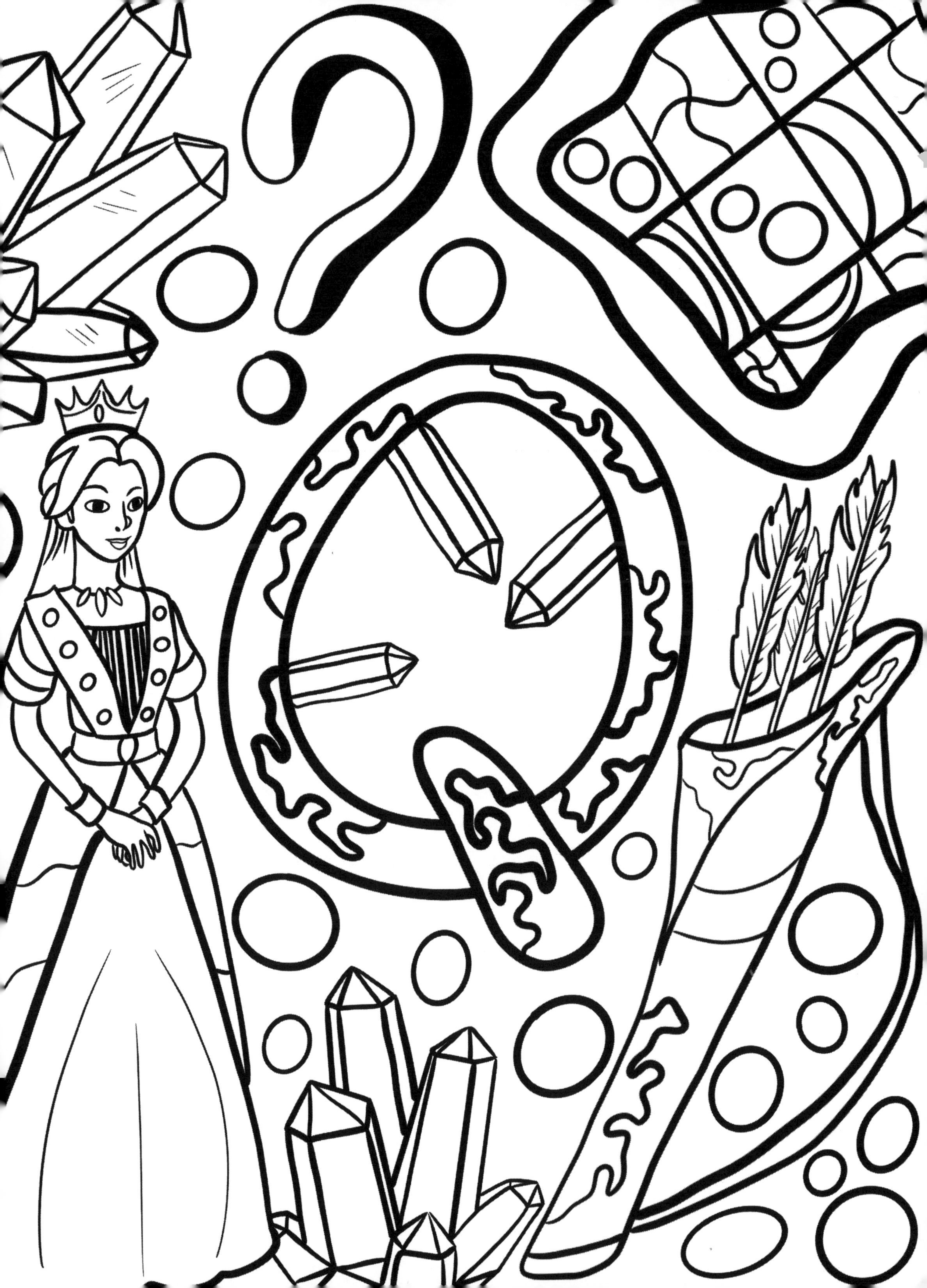

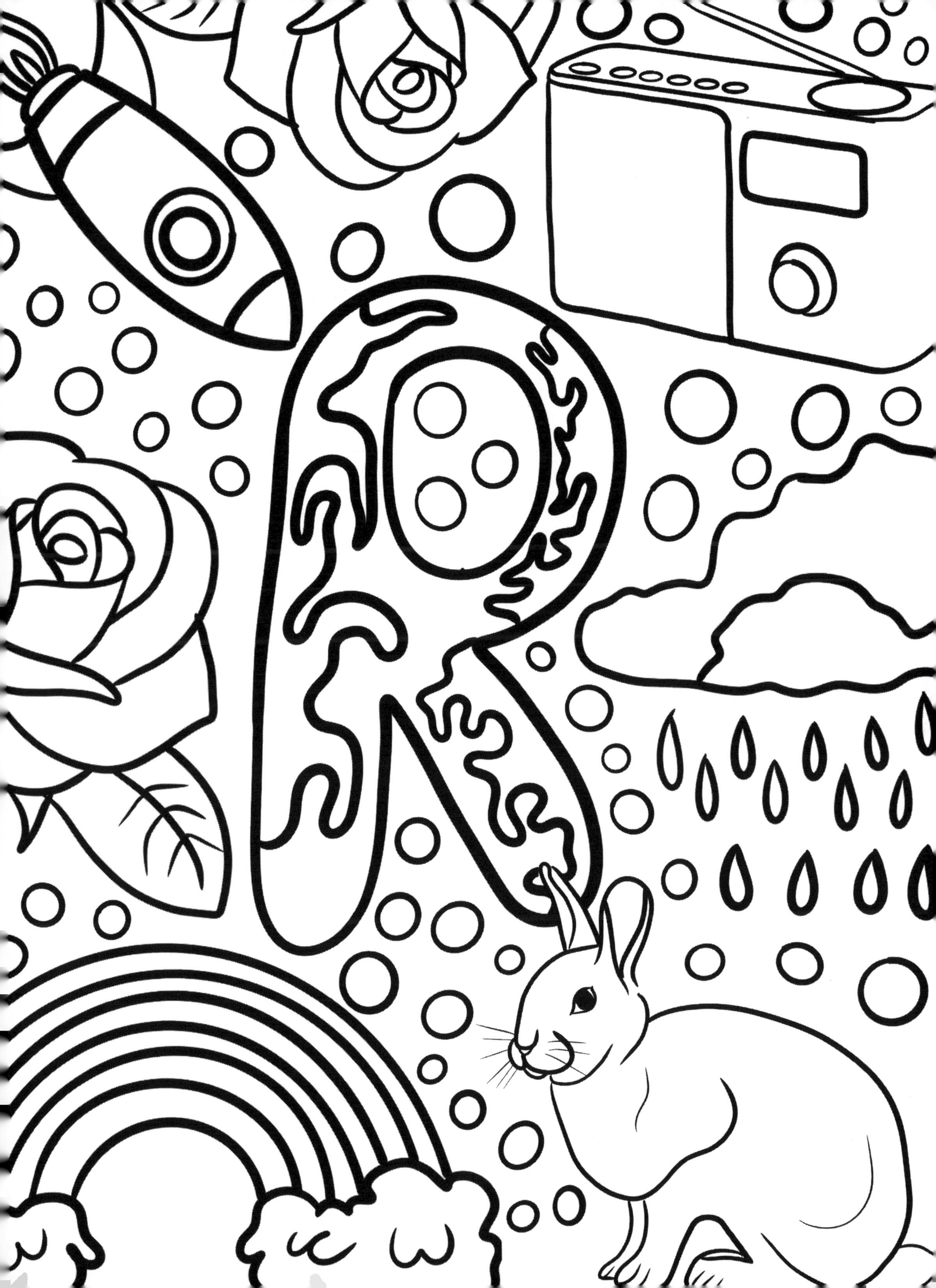
R

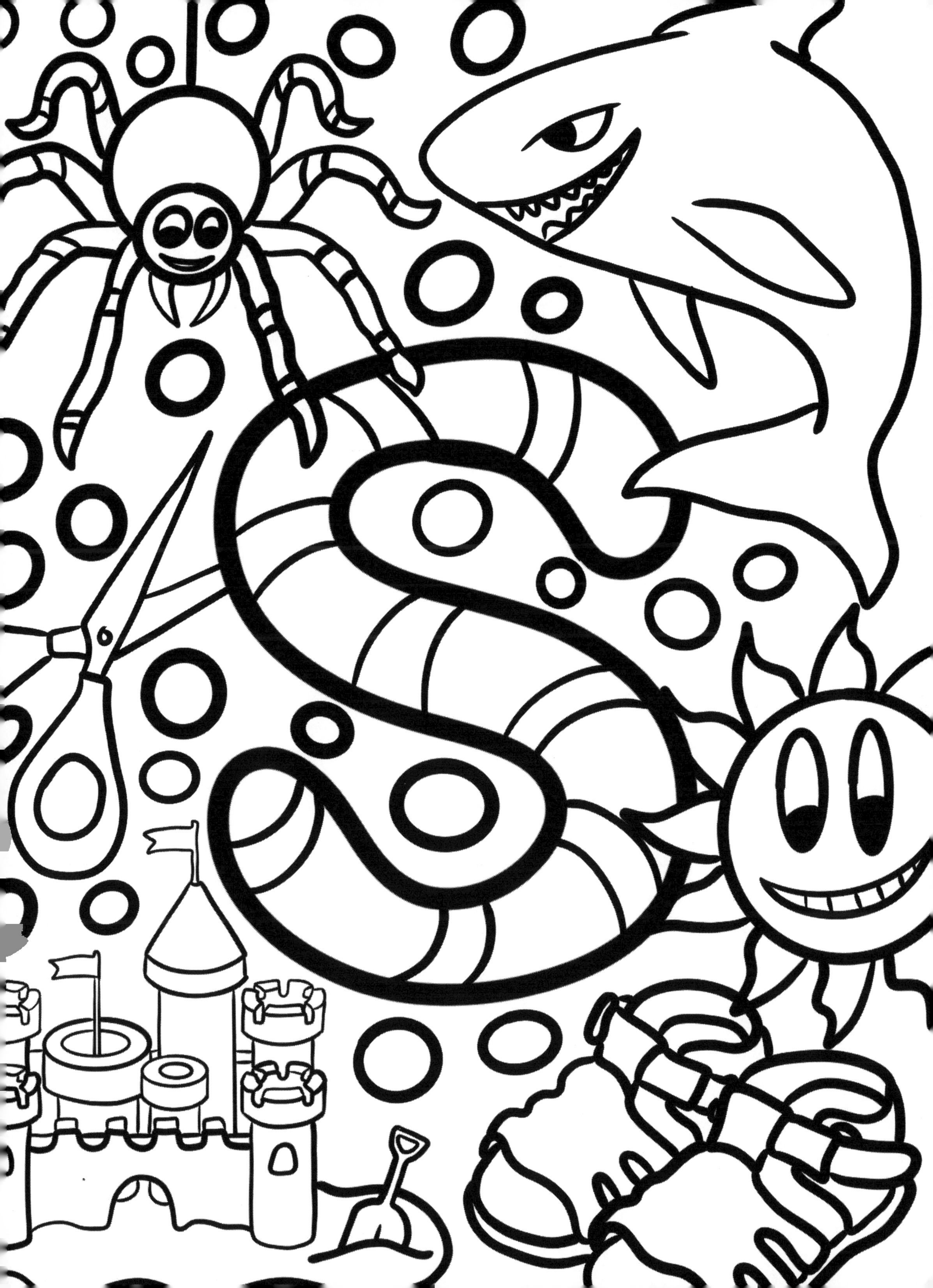

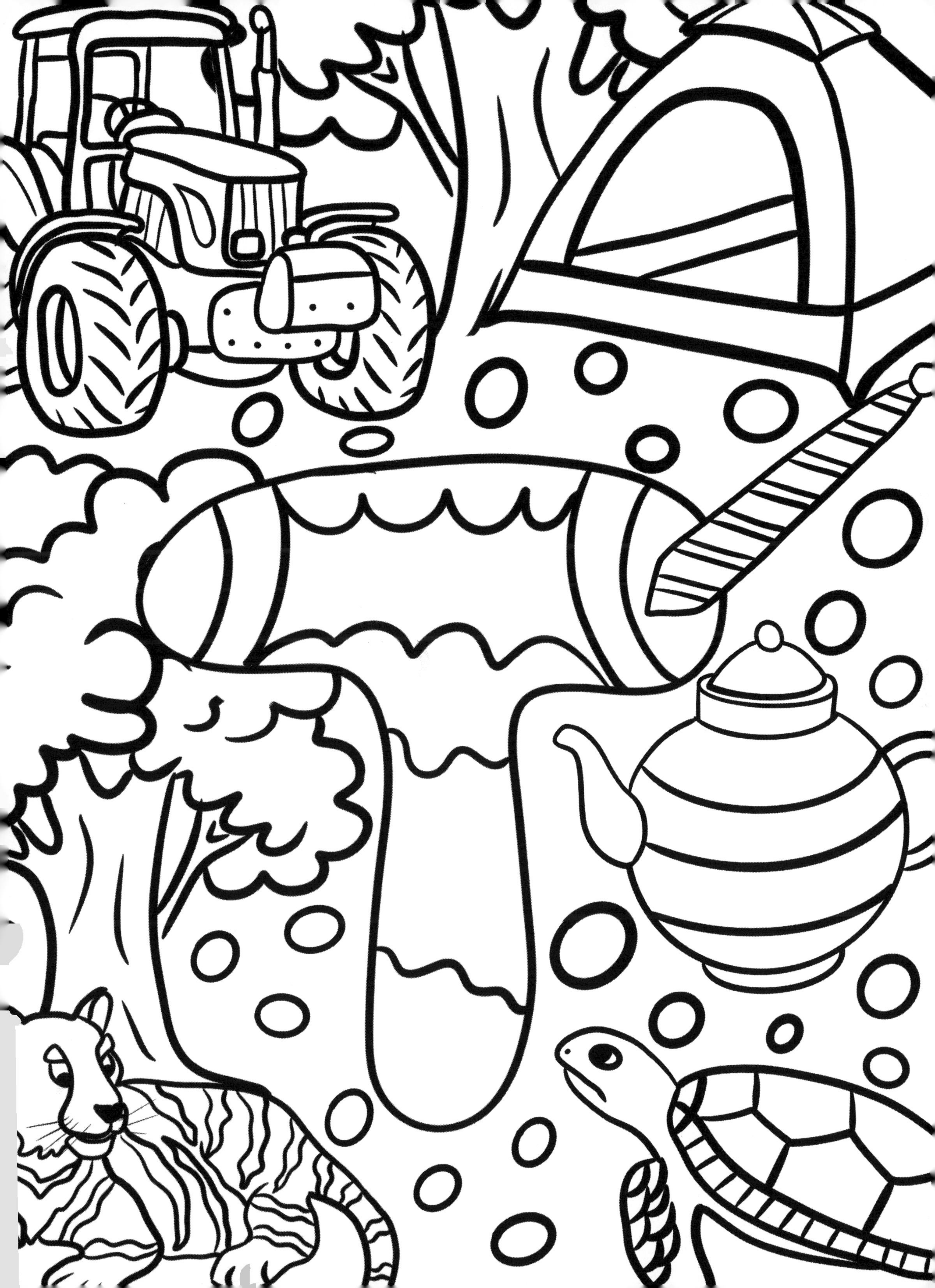

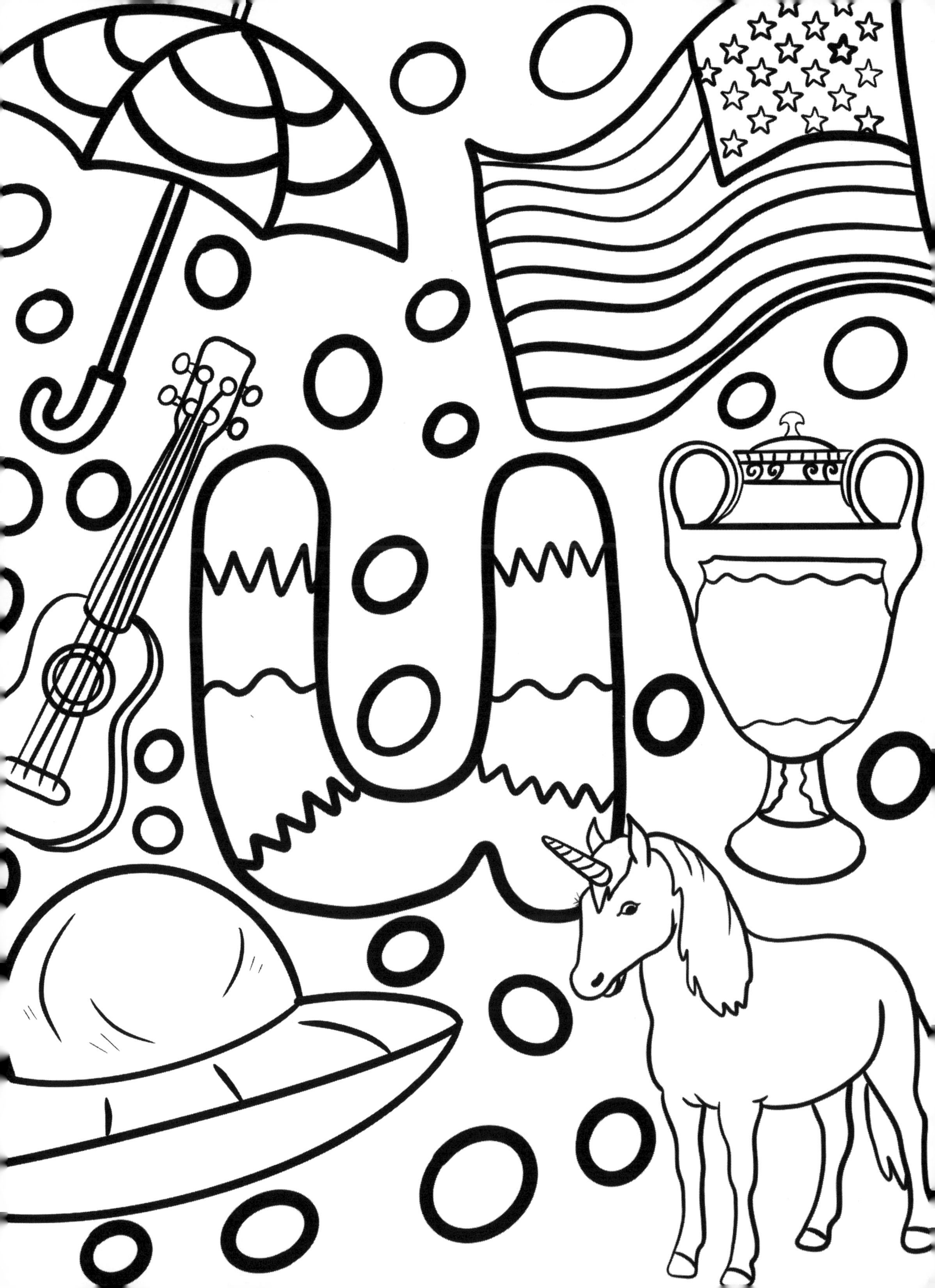

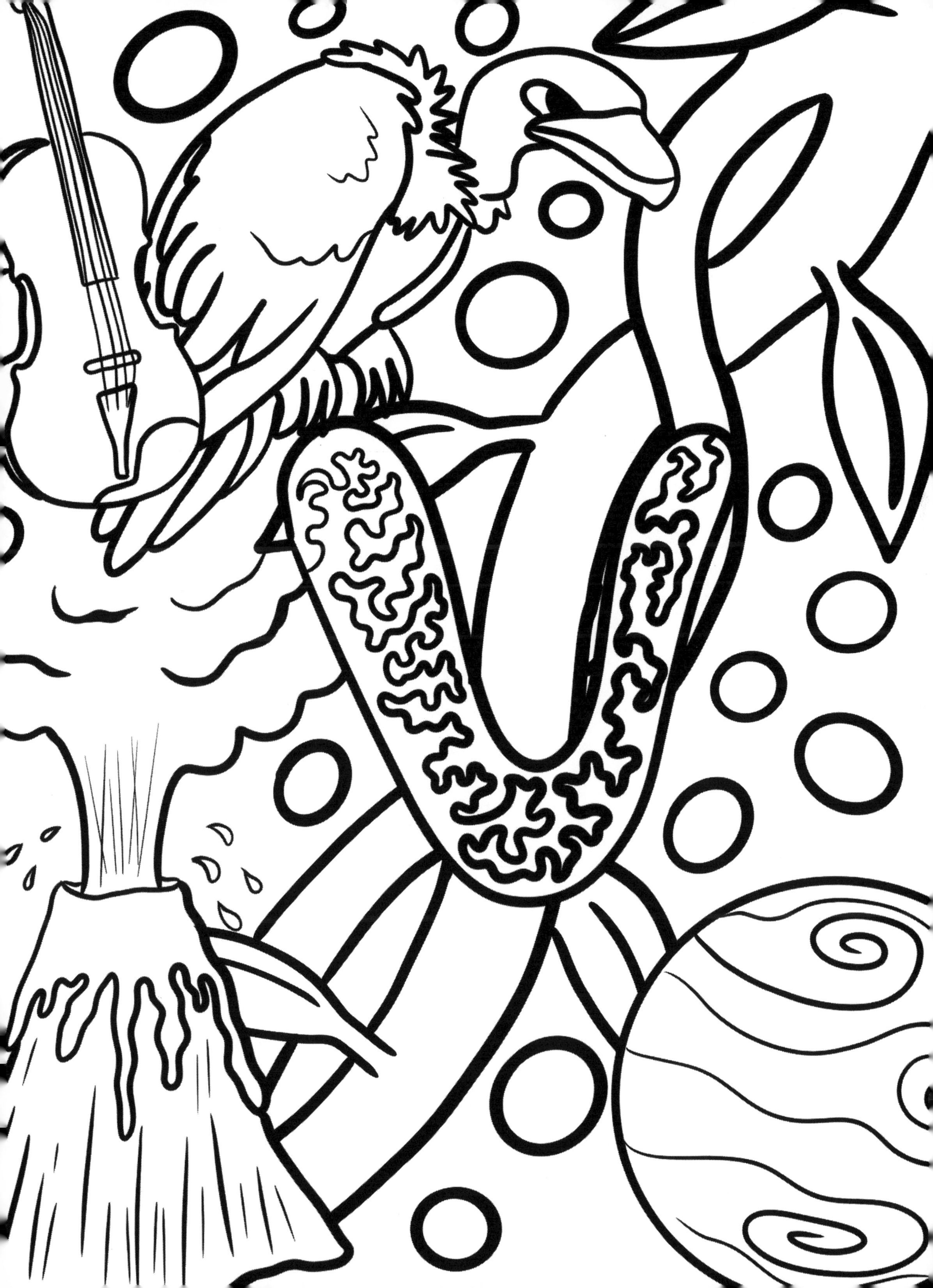

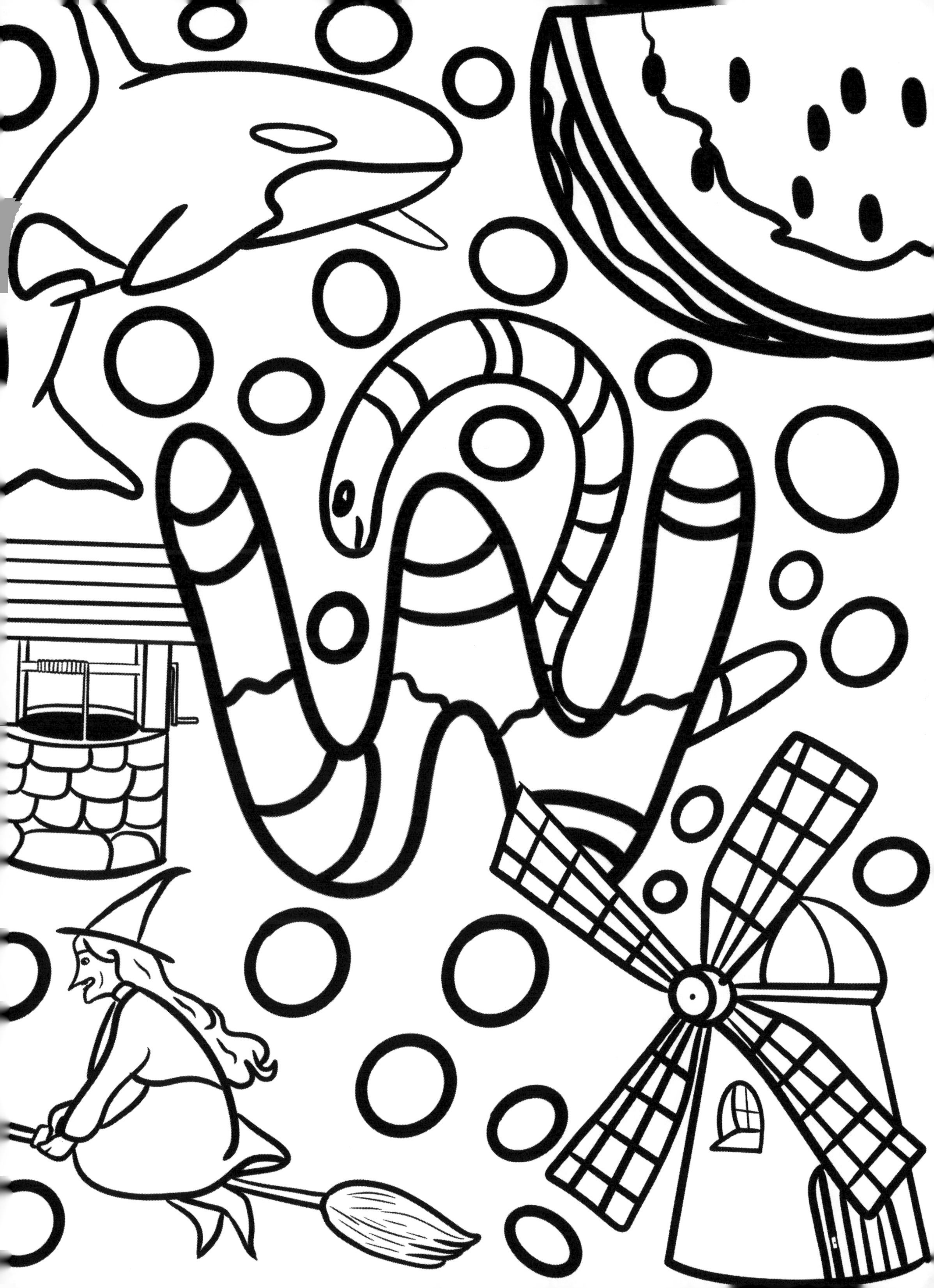

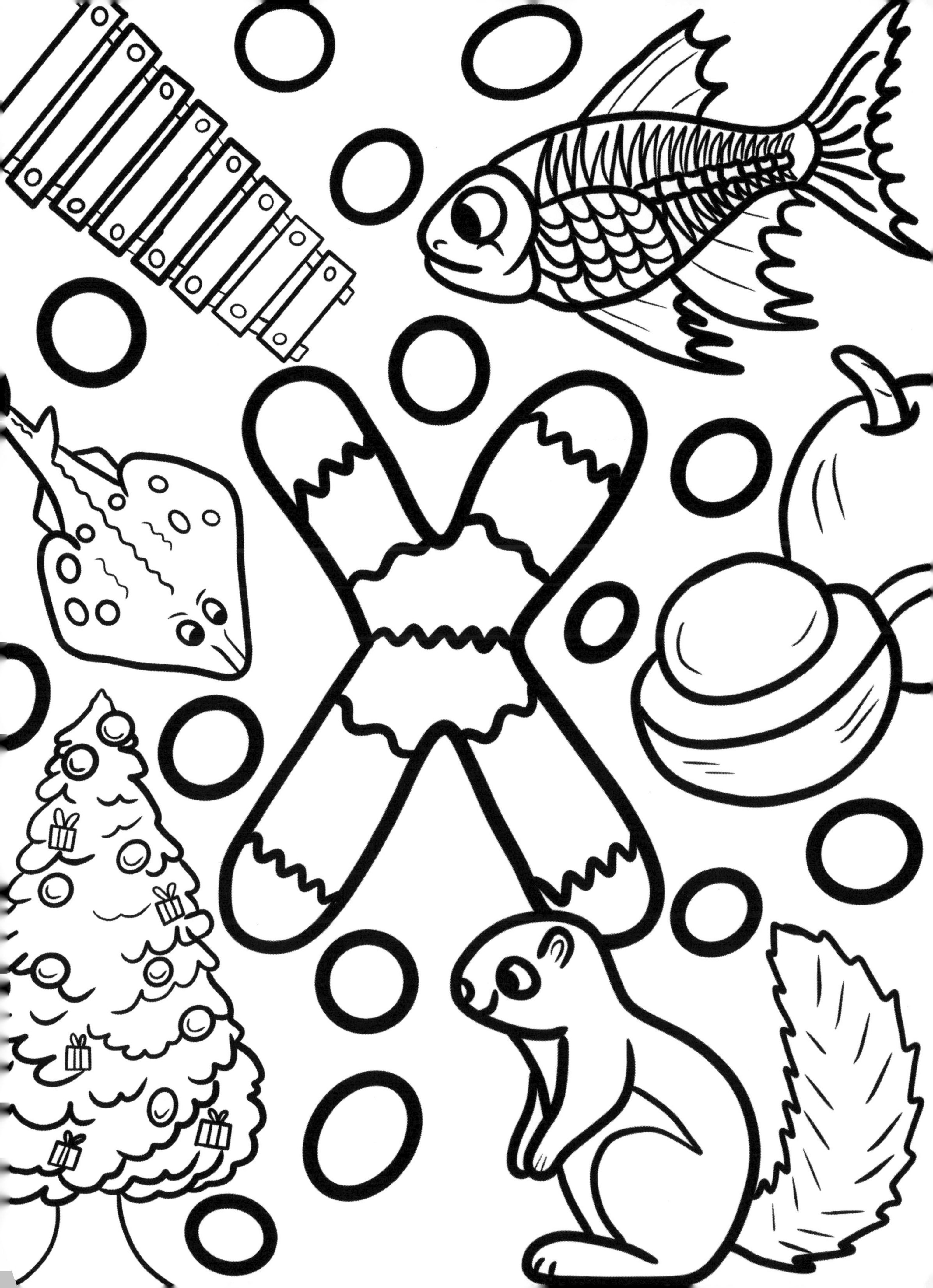

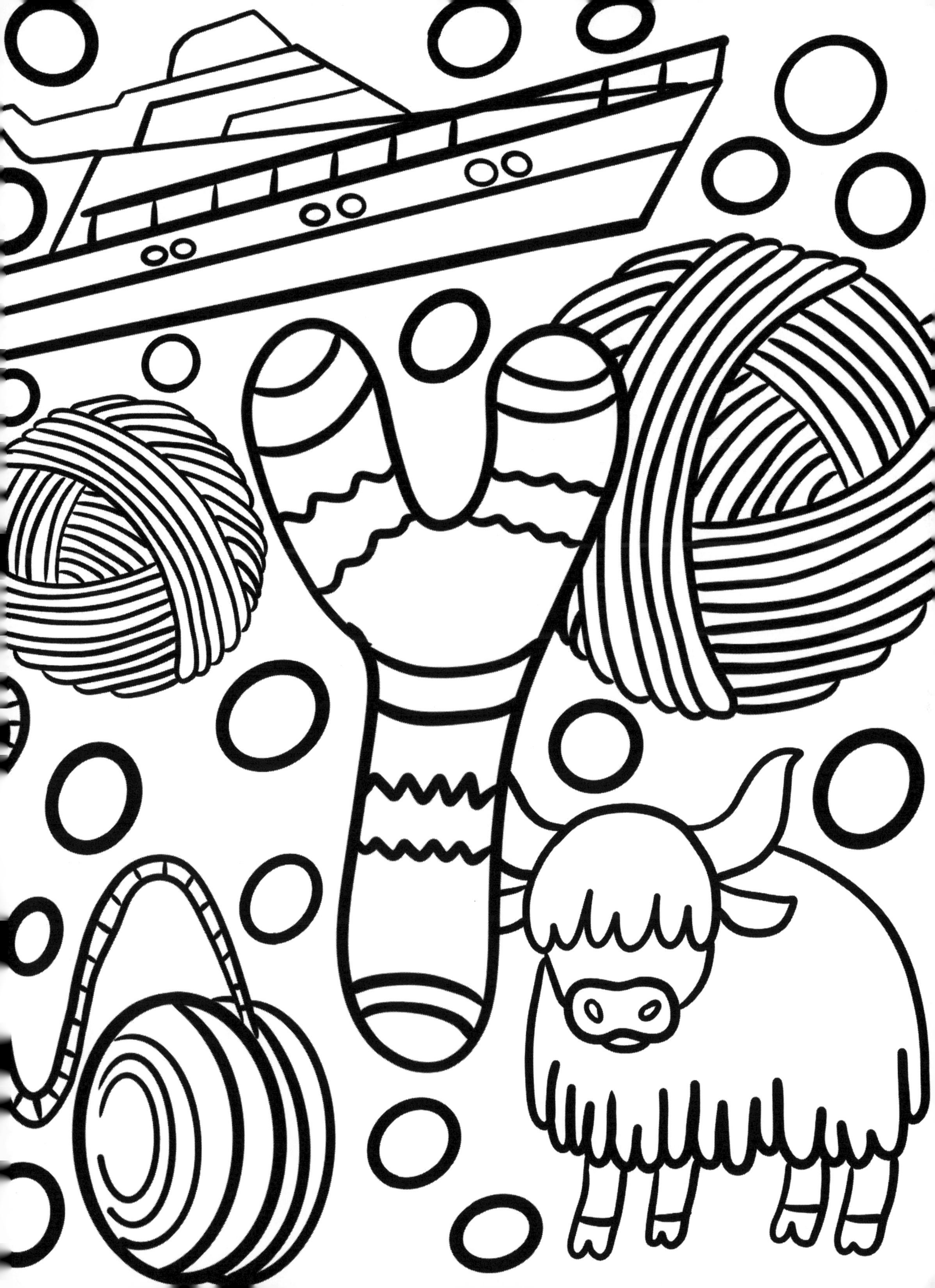

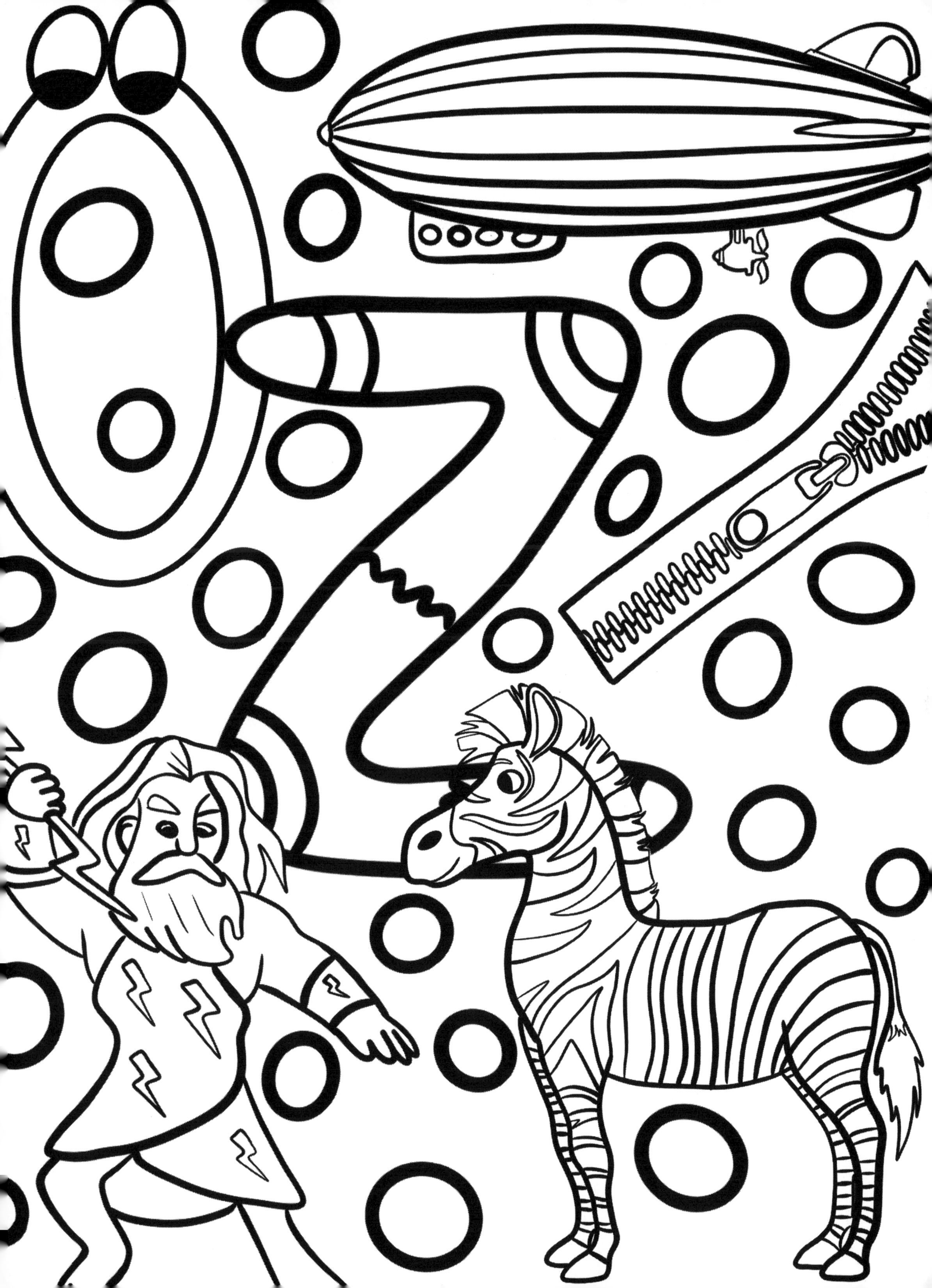

Printed in Great Britain
by Amazon

85306865R00032